MYTHOLOGY
AROUND THE WORLD

NORSE
MYTHS

by Eric Braun

Consultant:
John Lindow
Professor Emeritus
Department of Scandinavian
University of California, Berkeley

CAPSTONE PRESS
a capstone imprint

Fact Finders Books are published by Capstone Press,
1710 Roe Crest Drive, North Mankato, Minnesota 56003
www.mycapstone.com

Library of Congress Cataloging-in-Publication Data
Names: Braun, Eric, 1971– author.
Title: Norse Myths / by Eric Braun.
Description: North Mankato: Capstone Press, 2019. |
Series: Fact Finders: Mythology Around the World
Identifiers: LCCN 2018010994 (print) | LCCN 2018020438 (ebook) |
ISBN 9781515796046 (library binding) | ISBN 9781515796183 (paperback) |
ISBN 9781515796114 (eBook PDF)
Subjects: LCSH: Mythology, Norse—Juvenile literature.
Classification: LCC BL860 (ebook) | LCC BL860 .B673 2018 (print) | DDC 293/.13—dc23
LC record available at https://lccn.loc.gov/2018010994

Editorial Credits
Editor: Jennifer Huston
Production Artist: Kazuko Collins
Designer: Russell Griesmer
Media Researcher: Morgan Walters
Production specialist: Kathy McColley

Photo Credits: Alamy: Chronicle, 17, dieKleinert, 13, Ivy Close Images, 15, 20, 21, 25, 28, Lebrecht
Music and Arts Photo Library, 23, 27; Bridgeman Images: The Stapleton Collection, 6; North Wind
Picture Archives, 9, 19; Shutterstock: Fotokostic, 14, G.roman, (lightning) 1, cover, Igor Zh., 29,
Lukasz Szwaj, (paper texture) design element throughout, Madredus, (grunge) design element
throughout, Nejron Photo, 5, photocell, (plate) design element throughout, RaZZeRs, (flare) 1, cover,
Santi0103, design element throughout, T.SALAMATIK, (rain texture) design element throughout,
Vuk Kostic, 11, vukkostic91, Cover

Printed and bound in the United States of America.
122018 001373

TABLE OF CONTENTS

CHAPTER 1

THE CULTURE OF THE ANCIENT NORSE PEOPLE

Many people think of the Vikings as fierce warriors who raided foreign lands. In truth, the Vikings were a rather small group of Norsemen—people from Norway, Sweden, and Denmark. Most Norsemen were farmers and herdsmen. They grew grains and vegetables and raised cattle, goats, sheep, and pigs. So while all Vikings were Norsemen, not all Norse people were Vikings.

The Norse included various tribes of people living throughout northern Europe between about 1000 BC and AD 1000. These groups were not connected and likely didn't know one another. Even so, they did share certain **traits**. They **smelted** iron ore and made it into tools and cookware. They also had a rich tradition of preserving history through storytelling.

DID YOU KNOW?

For centuries Italian explorer Christopher Columbus has been credited with "discovering" North America in 1492. But historians now believe that Viking explorer Leif Eriksson landed in what is now Canada nearly 500 years before Columbus.

trait—a quality or characteristic that makes one person or animal different from another

smelt—to melt ore so that the metal can be removed from the rock

Viking longships had square sails and often had dragons or snakes carved into the front of the ship.

LIFE ON THE SEAS

The Norse people were also the greatest shipbuilders of their time. Their narrow wooden boats were powered by both sails and oars. These ships were quick and nimble, and the Norsemen used them to travel around the Baltic Sea and later much farther. They journeyed as far as northern Africa to trade. One of the most important products the Norsemen offered were furs from their homeland, which were highly valued. They also traded ivory from walrus tusks and iron for things such as silk, glass, and silver.

In the late AD 700s, some of the Norsemen began to change their approach to acquiring goods. They realized that the **monasteries** in the British Isles were easy targets for raiding. The monasteries were wealthy and not well defended. Plus they sat on coastlines where quick attacks and getaways would be easy. In AD 793 these Norse raiders attacked a monastery off the coast of northeastern England. These raiders became known as Vikings, and this attack marked the beginning of the Viking Age.

At first the Vikings staged attacks along coastal areas, but over time they began to strike farther inland. They began to settle in these lands as well. By the mid-800s, Vikings had built settlements in much of the British Isles as well as mainland Europe. They later settled in Iceland, where few people lived. By the late AD 900s they had settled in Greenland too.

The Vikings were fierce raiders and warriors, but they did not have horns on their helmets.

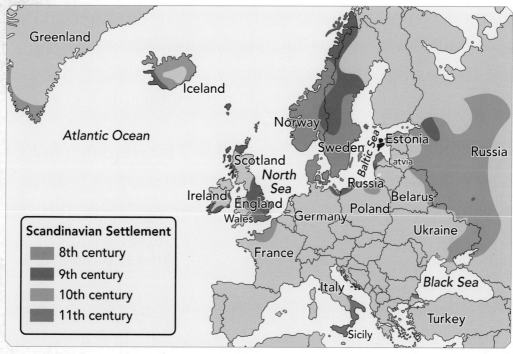

Present-day boundaries shown for context only.

Over time, weaker communities in Europe grew into powerful kingdoms that were not so easy for the Vikings to raid. In 1066 England's king, Harold Godwinson, defeated an invasion by Norwegian forces, ending the Viking Age.

monastery—a group of buildings where monks live and work

RELIGION

As the Norse people settled throughout Europe, they eventually took on the Christian religion. But before that, the Norse people believed in many gods. Although the Norse tribes were different from one another, their gods and myths were quite similar.

The Norse myths were passed down by word of mouth, so few written accounts of their gods and stories survive. The main texts are the *Prose Edda* and the *Poetic Edda*. An Icelandic historian wrote the *Prose Edda* around AD 1220. The *Poetic Edda,* a group of early Norse poems, dates from around AD 1270.

The Norse myths tell of great heroes, courageous battles, and gods communicating with humans. Life in Scandinavia was hard. Food and farming land were scarce, and loyalty and trust within tribes was extremely important. Many tales describe dishonesty, a lack of loyalty, and fighting within families. The myths, which storytellers often changed, reflected the hopes and fears of the people.

NORSE RITUALS

The Norse people built few temples. Ceremonies were held in **chieftains'** halls or outside. Most ceremonies involved thanking the gods, or asking them for good treatment or victory in battle. These ceremonies were usually held in connection with feasting.

In battle there were fierce warriors called berserkers and wolfskins. *Berserk* may mean "bear shirt" or "bare shirt." This suggests that these warriors either fought wearing bearskins or without a shirt or armor. They fought with such fury that the phrase *going berserk* comes from these warriors.

chieftain—the leader of a clan or tribe

CHAPTER 2

THE CREATION OF THE WORLD AND THE NORSE GODS

According to Norse mythology, before the world began, two opposite elements existed—fire and ice. There was a great dark opening between them. The first living being was a frost giant named Ymir. Ymir was formed from the drips of ice that melted in the heat of the fire.

The Aesir tribe of warrior gods, including their leader Odin, were **descendants** of these giants. Believing he was their enemy, Odin and his brothers killed him. From Ymir's body, Odin and his brothers built the universe, which consisted of nine worlds. The world where humans lived was called Midgard.

THE FIRST HUMANS

With the world established, Odin and his brothers began creating people. They found two logs on the seashore and breathed life into them. According to Norse mythology, all humans on Earth are descendants of these first two people. Their names were Ask and Embla.

descendants—all the relatives who trace their family roots back to one person
mortal—human; referring to a being who will eventually die

The Aesir gods battle against the frost giant Ymir.

Many other gods followed Odin and his brothers, including a separate tribe known as the Vanir gods. All the gods had humanlike qualities and feelings, such as anger, jealousy, and love. Unlike gods in some other traditions, the Norse gods were **mortal**, meaning they would not live forever.

Aesir God Family Tree

Most of the gods are descendants of the evil frost giant Ymir or a magical cow named Audhumla. Buri, the first of the Aesir gods, sprang to life out of a block of ice that Audhumla licked.

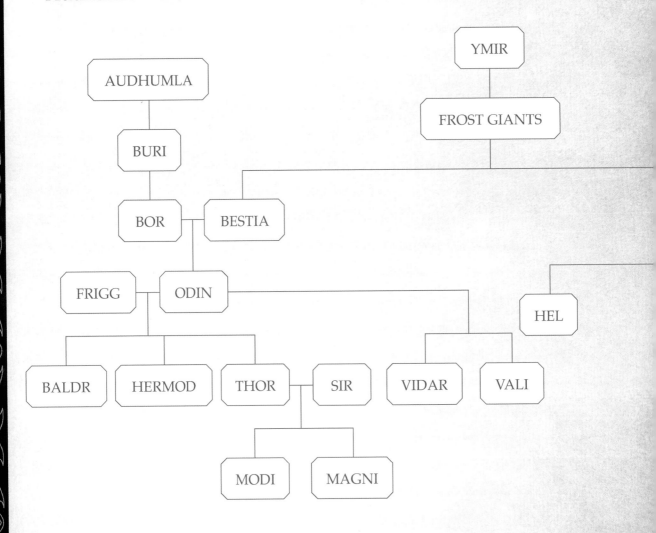

symbolize—to stand for or represent something else

shape-shift—to change into another animal or object

ODIN

Odin, the leader of the Aesir gods, **symbolized** power and strength. As the god of war, he was armed with his spear, which never missed its target. Odin was also a god of magic and could **shape-shift,** or turn into other people or creatures. He was always searching for knowledge and even gave up one of his eyes for wisdom.

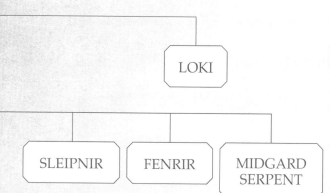

LOKI

SLEIPNIR   FENRIR   MIDGARD SERPENT

Odin had two ravens that flew around the universe gathering information.

DID YOU KNOW?

Odin had an eight-legged horse named Sleipnir that could fly. Sleipnir was a gift from Odin's frost giant blood brother, Loki.

FRIGG

Odin's wife, Frigg, was the goddess of marriage, love, fertility, and the household. She was also very wise and could see into the future.

BALDR

Baldr was the thoughtful, generous, and wise son of Odin and Frigg. He was also the god of light, beauty, joy, and innocence.

THOR

Thor, the son of Odin and Frigg, was the god of thunder and storms. Thor was a powerful god and was famous for killing giants. Thor is almost always pictured with his hammer, which would strike its target every time he threw it. Then it would return to him like a boomerang.

Thor enjoys fighting giants with his hammer, which he called Mjölnir.

LOKI

Loki was actually a frost giant, but he and Odin became blood brothers. Because of that, Loki was considered one of the gods, and he often helped them. But he was also a troublemaker who caused many problems for the gods. Loki's most important characteristic was his ability to shape-shift, which he often did to cause mischief.

HEL

Hel, the goddess of the Underworld, ruled over the dead who did not die in battle.

VALHALLA

Valhalla, or the "hall of the fallen," was the greatest hall in Asgard, the world of the gods. It was where Odin kept the dead warriors that he believed were worthy of dwelling with him. They were the ones who showed the greatest courage and skill in battle. According to myth, female spirits called Valkyries chose the heroes who were killed in battle and took them to Valhalla.

the Valkyries

NJÖRD

Njörd was the Vanir god of the sea and wind. Sailors would pray to him for calm waters and a safe journey. Njörd was also the father of Frey and Freya.

FREY

Frey was a Vanir god of plants. He had a boat that could be folded into a pocket and a boar that could fly. But his most important possession was his sword, which could swing itself and would always strike its enemy.

FREYA

Freya was the goddess of love, beauty, magic, war, and death. Some myths say she welcomed dead warriors into her heavenly field, Folkvang. There, she prepared them for Ragnarök, the final battle between the gods and giants at the end of the world.

YGGDRASIL AND THE NINE WORLDS

The ancient Norse people believed there were nine worlds in the universe. The nine worlds were all connected by a great ash tree known as Yggdrasil. The gods created a wall around Midgard to protect humans from the frost giants. They also built the flaming Rainbow Bridge between Midgard and Asgard. A large snake known as the Midgard Serpent surrounded all of Midgard.

YGGDRASIL—THE WORLD TREE

ASGARD:
Home of the Aesir gods

Rainbow Bridge

Midgard Serpent

MIDGARD:
Home of the humans

VANAHEIM:
Home of the Vanir gods

ALFHEIM:
Home of the elves

JÖTUNHEIM:
Home of the frost giants

MUSPELHEIM:
Home of the fire giants

NIFLHEIM:
Land of ice and mist

SVARTALFHEIM:
Home of the dwarves

HEL:
World of the dead

CHAPTER 3

THE STORIES

Life for the Norse people was harsh and full of danger, and their myths reflected that. Many stories were filled with violence and death. The gods had human emotions such as love, anger, jealousy, and fear. They made mistakes and fought with each other—just like humans.

BALDR'S DEATH

Many of the Norse myths revolve around Loki's mischief. In one story Baldr, the son of Odin and Frigg, began to have terrible dreams that he was going to die. When he told the other gods about his dreams, they discussed what the dreams meant. All the gods loved Baldr. They didn't want to believe that his death was near.

After meeting with the other gods, Odin rode Sleipnir down to the Underworld. There he consulted with a woman who could see the future. She told them what they all feared—Baldr was going to die.

What could they do? Frigg went around to all things in the universe—living and nonliving—and made them promise not to harm Baldr. Everything promised, from stones to birds, from fire to water to snakes. Even diseases made the promise. None of them would harm Baldr.

With all the attention being paid to Baldr, Loki became jealous. He disguised himself as an old woman and spoke to Frigg. He asked about Baldr, and Frigg told him of the promises she had received from all things.

Loki asked, "Did *everything* make this promise?"

Frigg drove all over the universe making sure that nothing would harm her son.

All except one little mistletoe, Frigg admitted. It was too young to make such a promise. With that, Loki left and found the mistletoe. He made poisoned darts out of it, and then, no longer in disguise, he returned to the gods.

Because they thought everything had promised not to hurt Baldr, the gods believed he was **invincible**. They decided to make a game of throwing things at him. Everything they threw, even stones, bounced off Baldr without hurting him. Then Loki suggested throwing his darts at Baldr. He didn't tell anyone they were made from the mistletoe. Worse yet, he convinced Baldr's blind brother, Höd, to throw the first dart. With Loki guiding his hand, Höd threw the mistletoe dart and killed Baldr.

Baldr is killed by a poisoned dart.

invincible—impossible to defeat

The gods were desperate to save Baldr. Another of Odin's sons, Hermod, went to Hel and asked her to release Baldr from the Underworld. She said she would do so only if everything in the universe cried for Baldr. The gods sent messengers throughout the universe to spread the word. Everything cried for Baldr—everything but one giantess, Thökk, who was really Loki in disguise. Since Thökk did not weep, Baldr remained with Hel in the Underworld.

Hermod bows before Hel and asks her to return Baldr to the living.

The Gods Take Revenge

Even though Loki tricked Höd into killing Baldr, the gods invited Loki to a feast. After all, Loki and Odin were still blood brothers. But when people at the feast praised the cooks, Loki became jealous and killed one of them. He went on to insult each god and goddess in cruel ways.

Fed up with Loki's bad behavior, the gods chased him into the forest. There he turned himself into a salmon and hid in a stream. But the gods spun a net and used it to capture him. Loki was sneaky and kept getting away, but finally the gods captured him.

Thor carried Loki into a cave. The gods tied up Loki and then caught a snake. They attached the snake above Loki's head so that **venom** dripped onto his face. Loki's wife, Sigyn, held a bowl under the dripping venom to protect him. But when the bowl was full she had to run off to empty it. While she was away, the poisonous venom burned Loki's eyes, nose, and mouth, and he squirmed in pain. Loki remained tied up until the time of Ragnarök, the last great battle.

venom—a poisonous liquid produced by some snakes when they bite

A crowd gathers to watch as Sigyn catches venom from a snake before it drips onto Loki.

Thor's Duel with Hrungnir

One day the mighty giant Hrungnir boasted that his horse was faster than Odin's magical steed, Sleipnir. So Odin challenged him to a race. The two raced their horses throughout Jötunheim, with Hrungnir chasing after Odin. They kept racing all the way up to Asgard, the world of the gods.

Hrungnir never caught up to Odin and Sleipnir, but the gods invited the giant to feast with them. However, Hrungnir was soon boasting again.

Eventually the gods grew tired of his boasts, so they called for Thor, who was off fighting giants elsewhere. Thor returned and raised his hammer to kill Hrungnir. But Hrungnir pointed out that he had no weapon to defend himself. He said it would be cowardly to kill an unarmed opponent. Instead he challenged Thor to a duel. Thor accepted.

whetstone—a stone for sharpening tools and weapons

flint—a hard gray rock that produces sparks when struck by metal

When the time came for their duel, Hrungnir went to the field where they were to fight. Then he saw lightning and heard thunder booming across the sky. Thor was approaching in his chariot. Hrungnir threw his **whetstone**, his chosen weapon, and Thor threw his hammer. The two weapons met in mid-air. The giant's whetstone struck Thor in the head and exploded, sending pieces of stone all over Earth. According to the story, this became the source of all the **flint** in the world. Thor's hammer then struck Hrungnir in the head, killing him.

Thor defeats the giant Hrungnir during a duel.

CHAPTER 4

THE END OF THE WORLD

The Norse people believed that the nine worlds of Yggdrasil came to an end during a final battle known as Ragnarök. According to the myths, Odin and the other gods knew Ragnarök was coming. They just didn't know when it would happen.

CALLED TO WAR

Just prior to Ragnarök, humans became more and more evil to one another. They fought great wars and even killed their own brothers and fathers. Winter continued for three straight years.

Plunged into darkness, Yggdrasil, the world tree, shook violently. The Midgard Serpent came out of the ocean and caused enormous waves and flooding.

At the same time, the evil wolf Fenrir broke free. The gods had chained him up to keep the world safe. Fenrir galloped across Midgard with his lower jaw dragging the ground and his upper jaw in the sky. He ate everything in his path, including the sun.

Loki was freed from the cave where he had been held and joined the frost giants. The fire giants came from the world of Muspelheim. As they crossed the Rainbow Bridge, it crumbled behind them. Heimdall, the god who stood guard at Asgard, blew his horn to warn the gods that they were being invaded.

During Ragnarök, the gods battled the giants as well as evil creatures, such as Fenrir and the Midgard Serpent.

Odin, Thor, and the other gods put on their armor. The giants were determined to destroy Asgard and the entire universe, but the gods fought back. During Ragnarök, the fire giant Surt sprayed flames all over the universe. The battle between the gods and the giants raged amid the flames until nearly everyone died. Loki and Heimdall battled each other for a long time. In the end both were killed. Fenrir killed the powerful Odin. Odin's son, Vidar, killed the wolf to avenge his father's death.

When a great battle raged between Thor and the Midgard Serpent, Thor killed the snake with a mighty blow from his hammer. But as Thor walked away from the Midgard Serpent's body, the snake's venom splattered all over him and killed him.

A New Beginning

As Ragnarök came to an end, the ruined land sank into the sea, leaving only silence and darkness. It was just as it had been at the beginning of time. Eventually a new world arose. It was green and beautiful.

The Norse believed that a new world arose after the destruction of Ragnarök.

Odin's sons, Vidar and Vali, survived Ragnarök and made it to this new world. Thor's sons Modi and Magni were also there. Baldr rose up from the Underworld. Two humans named Lif and Lifthrasir had hidden in the branches of the Yggdrasil tree and survived Ragnarök. They soon began to repopulate the world.

This story shows that the Norse people believed the world, and life, ran in **cycles**. Ragnarök was not really the end of the world. It was simply one point in a cycle of birth, life, and death that repeats over and over. The Norse people saw this cycle all around them—in day and night, the seasons, and all living things. Although the Norse myths were dark and violent, these cycles promised that a new beginning was sure to come.

THE LIGHT OF THE SKY

According to myth, Sol (which means Sun) and Mani (meaning Moon) were beautiful siblings. Each day Sol guided her chariot across the sky carrying the sun. Mani guided his chariot across the sky each night with the moon. To the ancient Norse people, this explained the story of day and night.

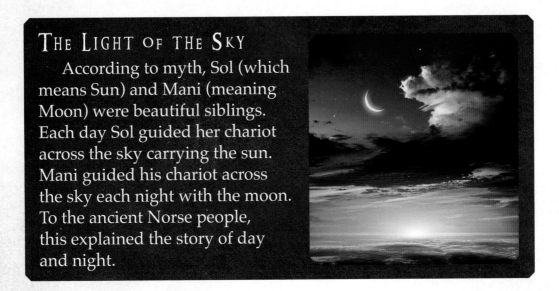

cycle—a set of events that happen over and over again

GLOSSARY

chieftain (CHEEF-tuhn)—the leader of a clan or tribe

cycle (SY--kuhl)—a set of events that happen over and over again

descendants (di-SEN-duhnts)—all the relatives who trace their family roots back to one person

flint (FLINT)—a hard gray rock that produces sparks when struck by metal

invincible (in-VIN-suh-buhl)—impossible to defeat

monastery (MAH-nuh-ster-ee)—a group of buildings where monks live and work

mortal (MOR-tuhl)—human; referring to a being who will eventually die

shape-shift (SHAYP-shift)—to change into another animal or object

smelt (SMELT)—to melt ore so that the metal can be removed from the rock

symbolize (SIM-buh-lize)—to stand for or represent something else

trait (TRAYT)—a quality or characteristic that makes one person or animal different from another

venom (VEN-uhm)—a poisonous liquid produced by some snakes when they bite

whetstone (WET-stone)—a stone for sharpening tools and weapons

READ MORE

Bowen, Carl. *Thor vs. the Giants: A Viking Graphic Novel*. Norse Myths. North Mankato, Minn.: Stone Arch Books, 2017.

Crossley-Holland, Kevin. *Norse Myths: Tales of Odin, Thor, and Loki*. Somerville, Mass.: Candlewick Press, 2017.

Napoli, Donna Jo. *Treasury of Norse Mythology: Stories of Intrigue, Trickery, Love, and Revenge*. Washington, D.C.: National Geographic Children's Books, 2015.

INTERNET SITES

Use FactHound to find Internet sites related to this book.

Visit www.facthound.com

Just type in 9781515796046 and go.

 Check out projects, games and lots more at
www.capstonekids.com

CRITICAL THINKING QUESTIONS

1. Why do you think the gods invited Loki back to feast with them after his tricks killed Baldr? Would you have done the same thing? Why or why not?

2. The Norse believed that Ragnarök could come any time. How do you think that affected their daily lives?

3. Norse myths often had themes of a harsh natural world, the importance of family loyalty, and issues such as love and jealousy. These reflected the real world that the Norse lived in. If myths were written about the world we live in today, what are some common themes that would show up in the stories?

INDEX